The Nonviolent Moment

Spirituality for the 21st Century

Mary Lou Kownacki, OSB

Pax Christi USA

The Nonviolent Moment

Spirituality for the 21st Century

Mary Lou Kownacki, OSB

Item No. 523-473
ISBN 0-9666285-8-6

03 04 05 06 4 3 2

Table of Contents

The Nonviolent Moment

Prayer for the
Decade of Nonviolence
for Children

I bow to the sacred in all creation.

May my spirit fill the world with beauty and wonder.
May my mind seek truth with humility and openness.

May my heart forgive without limit.
May my love for friend, enemy and outcast be without measure.
May my needs be few and my living simple.

May my actions bear witness to the suffering of others.
May my hands never harm a living being.
May my steps stay on the journey of justice.

May my tongue speak for those who are poor
without fear of the powerful.
May my prayers rise with patient discontent
until no child is hungry.

May my life's work be a passion for peace and nonviolence.
May my soul rejoice in the present moment.

May my imagination overcome death and despair
with new possibility.
And may I risk reputation, comfort and security
to bring this hope to the children.

Introduction

"What a society does to its children, its children will do to society," a Roman sage said.

What picture comes to mind when you read that quote?

Do you see long lines of hungry children in Africa? Or do you see a child eating a hot meal at a day care center?

Do you see children huddled together in bombed houses of Afghanistan? Or do you see children laughing and playing hide and seek together?

Do you see children watching television in empty apartments? Or do you see children being read to by volunteers in after-school programs?

Certainly the culture of violence seems to dominate. Children denied education, food, shelter, and medicine in two-thirds of the world. Millions of children sentenced to early death or robbed of full human lives. Even in the United States, the richest country in the world, we are waging a war on children: a violence-saturated media, children shooting children to settle minor conflicts. We have armies of children roaming the streets through most of the night armed with rage and alienation. Our schools are armed camps. And there is the hidden, institutionalized violence that kills both the bodies and spirits of our children. "I never knew we were supposed to eat three times a day," is what one eight-year-old boy said at the newly-opened Kids Cafe in inner-city Erie.

The culture of violence can numb. That's why I turn to the example of Venerable Maha Ghosananda, the renowned Buddhist monk who is a beacon of light for the suffering poor of Cambodia. When a writer asked him what he was currently doing, Ghosananda said he was working to get an international ban against land mines because in Cambodia so many people were getting killed or maimed by them.

When the writer asked how she could help, Ghosananda replied, "You must ask everyone you meet to sign a petition against land mines." Then he reached into the sleeve of his long orange robe, withdrew a petition and handed it to her.

The writer reflected on this simple gesture and concluded: "May we all be not more than one sleeve-length away from connecting our commitment to a peaceful heart to our commitment to a peaceful world."

Each of us can engage in a practice that, like Ghosananda's, links heart and hand.

For me, it is teaching poetry at the Inner-City Neighborhood Art House in my hometown, Erie, Pennsylvania. The Art House offers free lessons in the visual, performing, and literary arts to 800 at-risk children after school and during the summer.

These are poor children, many in violent surroundings. In a poetry class I taught, the assigned topic was "I Remember." One child wrote a poem about playing with a friend who was kidnapped before her eyes; another told about watching a stray pit bull tear her cat to shreds and being unable to help; a third wrote about someone breaking into her house and putting a gun to her head.

And yet...would it surprise you to learn that one of the most popular classes for both boys and girls at the

Neighborhood Art House is floral arrangement? That's because the "Flower Man," a local florist, comes to the Art House twice a week carrying dozens of flowers. The children gather around him, and he teaches them how to arrange orchids, roses, glads, carnations, and irises by color and shape and size in spectacular and surprising ways.

"My mom was so happy with the bouquet," a young boy said to the "Flower Man." "It was the first time we had real flowers in our house." To see the children running home through blighted neighborhoods splashing them with color and beauty is to understand why we opened the Art House.

I'm not saying a small Art House is a solution to violence, but it is a nonviolent step like Ghosananda's, a simple but strong statement for life. The Benedictine Sisters of Erie opened the Art House because we believe if we put art and beauty and values into the lives of children, we will reap soul.

Would children have a better chance to develop their potential if a few times a week they were exposed to a painting by Monet or Picasso or O'Keefe, not just the violent and sexually explicit images of MTV and BET?

Would their souls be richer if every day they listened to Bach and learned to play Mozart, if they heard the lyrics of Sandburg and Dickinson every day, not just DMX and Snoop Dog?

What if they memorized words that were inspiring or humorous rather than violent and nihilistic? "You are what you think," the Buddha said. What thoughts do you want running through your child's head? Which words do you think build sensitivity and self-respect? The violent, misogynist, anti-gay lyrics of Eminem, "shut up, bitch, you move again I'll beat the f___ out of you," or this from Langston Hughes:

Hold fast to dreams
For if dreams die
Life is a broken winged bird
That cannot fly.
Hold fast to dreams
For when dreams go
Life is a barren field
Frozen with snow.

What if our children developed self-confidence and self-esteem by performing in public and learning to play an instrument, painting pictures from inside themselves and dancing to *Swan Lake*? What if they learned to work with their peers for a common goal where all shared in the applause? Would this help instill compassion, empathy, tolerance? Would this dent the culture of violence?

Who knows? But I'd rather take a chance on something like an Art House than begin raising taxes for more juvenile detention centers.

Ten-year-old Johnny was one of our most talented students. He could act, write and create extraordinary works of art for a child his age. A well-known Erie artist was so impressed with Johnny's work that she was arranging for private lessons. For three years Johnny came to the Art House every day after school. One afternoon, in the middle of a class, his father came in and told him to get his coat and collect his framed art pieces hanging on the walls, they were leaving for Florida. Johnny started to cry. "I love it here," he said. "Please tell everyone 'thank you,'" he sobbed to Sister Anne, the director. "Do they have an art house in Florida?" he asked through tears as he walked out the door.

I don't know, Johnny, but they should. There should be a center for children in every neighborhood in every city. We cannot have enough safe places for children to go. "Nothing you do for children is ever wasted," Garrison Keillor said. It's time we believed him.

The United Nations has proclaimed 2001-2010 to be the "International Decade for the Culture of Peace and Nonviolence for the Children of the World." Pax Christi USA asked me to write a prayer for this special observance and then to write a commentary on the prayer itself. Let's keep children like Johnny in mind when we say the prayer and use this booklet for personal or group reflection. "Children are the living messages we send to a time we will not see," wrote John W. Whitehead. Can we embrace the children of the world in a way of love, compassion and justice so that the "time we will not see" is a time of nonviolence?

One more thing. What breaks my heart at the Art House is to see children, nine to 12 years old, acting way beyond their years. When their conversation is filled with sexual innuendo, when their mouths are foul and violent, when they swagger and take on pseudo-sophistication, I can forget that these are only children. But to see these streetwise kids get excited about dramatizing elementary school poems like "Mice" by Rose Flyman and "Sick" by Shel Silverstein and "Sometimes I Feel This Way" by John Ciardi...to hear them giggle and play, is to rediscover innocence. Theirs and mine.

"The catcher in the rye" is what 17-year-old Holden Caufield tells his little sister he wants to be, rejecting her suggestions of lawyer and scientist. Holden, the narrator and main character in Salinger's classic novel *The Catcher in the Rye*, wants to preserve innocence.

He tells his sister that he imagines thousands of small children playing in a field of rye. At the end of the field is a cliff and if the children in their play wander too close and fall, he would be there to protect them.

I confess that an adolescent Holden still lives in my 60-year-old body. I know we can't protect the children forever. But, my God, can we at least wait until the children turn 12 before we leave them alone to fly off the cliffs of innocence? Can we at least try to catch them before they drop into the abyss of sex and drugs and violence? Perhaps we could look at the "Decade of Nonviolence for Children" as a "catcher in the rye movement."

— Mary Lou Kownacki, OSB

The Call of Nonviolence

I bow to the sacred in all creation.

Bows are an important part of my monastic life. When the community gathers at morning, noon and evening to chant the liturgy of the hours, we stand and bow during each prayer period. That's at least three bows each time we gather. Close to 10 bows a day. About 70 bows a week. Nearly 3,700 bows a year.

On important feasts we process into the monastery chapel in two lines and at the altar we bow, two-by-two, to recognize the Christ in the Word, then turn and bow to each other, recognizing the sacred in our sister. With a slight nod of the head, we bow to each other when we pass in the monastery halls. And when we are going on a long journey we bow for the prioress' blessing. We bow and we bow and we bow until over the years the ritual becomes the reality.

Which is to say we are in a perpetual posture of reverence and vulnerability. Many people reach this holy posture without benefit of daily monastic practices. Remember Saint Francis, bending to kiss the leper. Or the saintly Father Zossima bowing before the belligerent Dmitri in the *Brothers Karamazov*. Or the newly-elected president of Haiti, Jean Bertrand Artistide, celebrating his inaugural by inviting the poor of Port-au-Prince to the Presidential Palace and then kneeling in front of a blind woman and feeding her. Or think of a mother bowing to tend to her child. A pre-school teacher bowing to lace her student's shoe. A white-haired man bowing to lift his new grandchild.

A Zen master says it this way: "People often ask me how the Buddhists answer the question, Does God exist?

"The other day I was walking along the river. The wind was blowing. Suddenly I thought, oh, the air really exists. We know that the air is there, but unless the wind blows against our face, we are not aware of it. Here in the wind I was suddenly aware, yes, it's really there.

"And the sun, too. I was suddenly aware of the sun, shining through the bare trees. Its warmth, its brightness, and all of this completely free, completely gratuitous. Simply there for us to enjoy.

"And without knowing it, completely spontaneously, my two hands came together, and I realized that I was making gasho (bowing). And it occurred to me that this is all that matters: that we can bow, take a deep bow. Just that. Just that."

To bow and to cower are not synonyms. A person who bows must first know how to stand. Such a person understands the teachings of the Hasidim that we should all have two pockets: in one is the message, "I am dust and ashes," and in the other, "For me the universe was made." Only when we recognize our place in the universe and accept it, can we bow. We bow to acknowledge that all life is a gift. We bow because we recognize the sacredness of everything we meet—be it a stone, a tree, a dandelion, a friend, an enemy.

In the Rule of Saint Benedict, the spiritual master tells us that the final degree of humility is to bow everywhere, field as well as chapel. A truly humble person is in harmony, transparent before all creation.

Once we possess the inner posture of bowing before

all that is, then it becomes impossible to harm any part of creation.

Is this the beginning or the final stage of the journey into nonviolence? Or is it both? It doesn't matter. Just practice bowing–inwardly and outwardly. Bow as you walk through the neighborhood. Bow to your children sometime. Or your students. Stop in front of a tree and make a profound bow. Bow when you pass the church. Look in the mirror and bow. Bow before the swinging door of a tavern.

And when you see a person you don't like, fall on your knees before them and touch the ground with your forehead. The children of the world are waiting and watching.

I bow to the sacred in all creation.

Reflection/Discussion Questions

1. What thoughts and feelings surfaced during the reading?

2. To whom would you find it easy to bow?
   To what? And why?

3. To whom would you find it difficult to bow?
   To what? And why?

4. Do you believe the sacred exists in all creation?
   Why or why not?

5. What would change in you and in your interactions with your environment if you committed to practicing bowing—inwardly and outwardly?

6. How do you think the practice of bowing to all creation would affect your practice of nonviolence?

Action Suggestions

1. Dialogue with your children about this concept of bowing to acknowledge the sacredness in all things. Practice bowing to each other and then share your feelings.

2. Commit to daily acknowledgment of the sacred in all by bowing outwardly and/or inwardly. Journal about your feelings and experiences (this does not need to be lengthy).

The Spirit of Nonviolence

*May my spirit fill the world
with beauty and wonder.*

May my spirit fill the world with beauty and wonder.

Look, children,
Hail-stones!
Let's rush out!
—Basho

For everything that lives is holy,
life delights in life.
—William Blake

So much depends
upon
a red wheel
barrow
glazed with rain
water
beside the white
chickens
—William Carlos Williams

One moment of pure seeing
is the beginning of liberation.
If you can see, for a moment,
one flower, one face, one dog,
as they are in themselves
and for themselves
you have begun to be free
enough to love.
—Amanda

Sit quietly,
doing nothing,
spring comes,
and the grass
grows by itself.
—Zen saying

Every day more precious will dawn
And loved faces turn dearer still.
—Robert Penn Warren

May my spirit fill the world with beauty and wonder.

Let the beauty we love
be what we do.
—Rumi

A morning glory at my window satisfies me
more than the metaphysics of books.
—Walt Whitman

Lovely snowflakes,
they fall
nowhere else!
—Zen saying

Let yourself
be silently drawn
by the stronger pull
of what
you really
love.
—Rumi

Let us save
birds in the sky
and old turtles.
—Emily Graham, 8

Falling Star

My name is Falling Star
I twinkle about the night sky
Many children wish on me
Once I fell in a hole
Darker than the heavens
But I wasn't afraid because
I gave myself light.
—Alla Meroshnik, 9

May my spirit fill the world with beauty and wonder.

Reflection/Discussion Questions

1. What thoughts and feelings surfaced during the readings?

2. When was the last time these feelings were present within you?

3. Recall and share a time when you were moved to express your thoughts and feelings in this manner.

4. What do you see as the connection between these readings and the development of a spirit of nonviolence?

Action Suggestions

1. Journal about those things that evoke feelings of reverence, awe and wonder.

2. Spend time with a child/children expressing in some art form, drawing, painting, clay, writing, those things in which they find beauty. Make the connection with these and the sacredness of all life.

*May my mind seek truth
with humility and openness.*

I admit to walking like someone barefoot on crushed glass when it comes to discussing truth. Very gingerly. The minute you try to nuance the search for truth, you start to sound dogmatic, as if you already possessed the pearl of great price. I prefer to enter the discussion on truth through stories that hint at the spirit of a truth seeker.

The first story tells about a person who is renowned for his wisdom and holiness. Whenever he was asked how he had become so enlightened he said, "I know what is in the Bible."

One day he had just given this answer to an inquirer when an exasperated voice shouted, "Well, what is in the Bible?"

"In the Bible," said the enlightened one, "there are two pressed flowers and a letter from my friend, Jonathan."

This is a wonderful story to keep in mind while praying, "May I seek truth with humility and openness." I mean, what a surprise ending. What a new way of looking at what makes for enlightenment. Like all of Jesus' parables, the holy man's response just wreaks havoc with all the "right" and "true" answers that we have stored in our heads. Answers we spew out with the certainty of a chief justice. The government, for example, is certain that the only way to preserve peace is to build more sophisticated weapons of war; the way to stop murder is to murder those who commit murder. The church has volumes of certainties including women can never be ordained and gays and lesbians can never express physical intimacy. The peace movement can be as dogmatic and inflexible about nonviolence and pacifism as those who rigidly support peace through military strength. So the first truth of the search for truth is "be open to surprise."

The next story tells of a seeker who went to visit a Holy One hoping for enlightenment. The Holy One invited the seeker into her cell and offered her a cup of tea. The seeker accepted the drink and watched as the Holy One filled her cup with tea and kept pouring. When she could take it no longer, she said, "The cup is overfull. No more will go into it." The Holy One replied, "Like the cup, you are full of your own truths, ideas and opinions. You cannot be enlightened until you first empty your cup."

If you had to draw a picture of a nonviolent spirit, an empty tea cup would suffice. Or a hollow gourd. Or, in the Christian tradition, an empty tomb. It takes a lifetime to empty yourself out of certain truths and cherished beliefs until only the mystery of God shines through. It is a tricky business to become such a void that all people, ideas and beliefs can find room in the empty space at your center. It is hard writing about something you do not yet possess, but this hospitable hollowness is so inviting when you see it radiate in a person. It's not that the person is without convictions; on the contrary, she or he often has the strongest sense of direction and the purest or simplest of truths on which to build a life. The difference is that such a person remains open to other truth and respectful of every person bearing different visions.

The Buddhist author and Nobel Peace Prize nominee, Thich Nhat Hanh, tells the third story. A father left his village on business and while he was gone bandits came and burned down the village and kidnapped his son. When the father returned he found a burned corpse near his home and thought it was the remains of his son. The father almost went mad with grief and, after an elaborate cremation ceremony, placed the ashes of his son in a beautiful velvet bag, which he carried with him always.

One day the son escaped from his kidnappers and arrived at his father's home at midnight. He knocked, and his father, who was holding the bag of his son's ashes, said, "Who is there?" The child answered, "It is me, papa. Open the door. It's your son." But the father was so certain that his son was dead that he told the boy to stop tormenting him and go away. The boy knocked and knocked, but the father never answered. He held the velvet bag closer and cried without ceasing. Finally the child left and the father and son never saw one another.

Every time I find myself hotly defending a cherished belief, I remember this story. Every time I find myself shouting my truth at an opposing idea, as if the volume of my defense makes it truer, I check for the velvet bag. Every time I refuse to read or listen to an opposing view, every time I mock or belittle another's truth, I become the guarded father.

Here the secret is dialogue. If the father had only asked for some detail that only the son would know—what was your nickname? How did we celebrate your birthday?– then truth could emerge. But the father chooses to cling to his truth–"My son is dead"–and locks himself away from new truth. He is unable and unwilling to respond when truth knocks on the door.

There is no great mystery to the seeking of truth. Parker Palmer defines truth as "an eternal conversation about things that matter, conducted with passion and discipline." How simple, how beautiful. How rare. And how terrifying.

Terrifying, because the door to truth is painful. Being stripped of any illusion–my friends will not betray me; the peace movement is not competitive; I am nonviolent; the church has a preferential option for the poor; the government's concern is justice–is a torturous letting go of cherished beliefs and hopes. The ego or false self is stripped away layer by layer until only darkness remains. Yes, the truth will set you free, but the price....See Gandhi, Jeannine Gramick, Charles Curran, Martin Luther King Jr., Dorothy Day, Phil Berrigan.

Which brings us to the last story. Three people on the search for truth heard that a holy hermit living at the edge of town had the key to understanding truth. The three went to visit the hermit and asked if she could help them unlock truth. The hermit said she could. "Well, then," said one of the seekers, "could you please turn the key and open the door of truth for us?" The hermit who had been listening with her eyes closed, suddenly opened them both and they were as wide and wild and ferocious as a tiger's.

"And once I open the door," she demanded, "just how far would you like to go into truth?"

The three seekers looked at each other and shifted uncomfortably. Finally, one of them said, "We'd like to go in, but not too far. Just far enough so we can say we've been there."

So, as far as I can tell, seeking truth has something to do with surprise, openness, letting go and walking into the jaws of a tiger.

May my mind seek truth with humility and openness.

Reflection/Discussion Questions

1. What thoughts and feelings surfaced during this reading?

2. Define truth.

3. How far are you willing to go in the search for truth?
   What truths do you really not want to know?
   How open are you to other truths?

4. What are the "truths" that you hold clutched in your "velvet bag"?

5. What would be the price for emptying your bag of those truths in order to become "hospitably hollow"?

Action Suggestions

1. Pray daily to seek truth with humility and openness. Journal about your feelings, experiences and what changes you are beginning to recognize in yourself.

2. Identify someone whose truth is different from yours and with whom it has been difficult to converse. Engage in dialogue in a nonviolent manner with respect and openness.
   How did it feel?
   Did it change the dynamics between you?
   Were you able to acknowledge that person's truth?
   Did your truth expand?

The Heart of Nonviolence

May my heart forgive
without limit.

M y favorite definition of God is Thomas Merton's: God is "mercy within mercy within mercy."

And I greatly admire those godlike figures who show mercy without limit, who forgive unconditionally. Jesus, crying his forgiveness while being tortured to death, comes to mind. Or Saint Stephen forgiving his stone-throwing killers. Or Gandhi reciting his mantra as his assassin sent a bullet into his heart.

On the other hand, though I pray to forgive without limit, I still wrestle with some questions: Why is it easier for me to forgive someone who has harmed me, more difficult to forgive those who have hurt my family, friends or innocent victims? Is it wrong to be guarded around those who have maligned me? Isn't it naïve and evidence of low self-esteem to just embrace a person who has repeatedly set out to harm me? How do I reconcile Jesus' invitation to forgive seventy times seven with the passage from John's gospel that reads: "He did not trust himself to them because he knew what was in their hearts." Are there horrific deeds that should never be forgiven? Genocide? Mass murder? Torture of women and children?

Not only do I have questions about forgiveness, but I also hold to a few maxims. First, only the person who has been wronged has the right to forgive.

Recently I read a remarkable story about forgiveness involving the young girl captured in the famous Vietnam War photo: nine-year-old Phan Thi Kim Phuc running naked down a road, her back afire from napalm. The young soldier, John Plummer, who organized and participated in the air strike on the village of Tang Bang in 1972 was haunted by the Pulitzer Prize-winning photo, which he saw shortly after the bombing raid.

Kim Phuc underwent plastic surgery, married, defected to Canada and became a spokesperson for UNESCO. Plummer returned home racked with guilt, divorced, turned to alcohol and then met his second wife, who led him to God and the ministry. Plummer said he thought about Kim Phuc every day and wanted to tell her how sorry he was but could not summon the courage to contact her.

In 1996 Kim Phuc was the main speaker at a special service at the Vietnam Veterans Memorial in Washington. Plummer went to the observance and heard Kim Phuc say that if she met the pilot of the plane she would tell him she forgives him and that they cannot change the past but she would hope they both could work together to build the future. Through friends Plummer got word to her that the soldier she wanted to meet was there. "She saw my grief, my pain, my sorrow," Plummer wrote. "She held out her arms to me and embraced me. All I could say was 'I'm sorry; I'm so sorry; I'm sorry' over and over again. At the same time she was saying, 'It's all right; It's all right; I forgive; I forgive.'" Kim Phuc and Rev. Plummer met many times after that and even worked together on a few projects. Kim Phuc, who lost two brothers in that 1972 bombing raid, now considers Plummer her brother. Plummer says, "She is the closest thing to a saint I ever met."

The second limit on forgiveness is that cheap forgiveness is worthless and probably harmful.

One of the most honest exchanges I've ever encountered in forgiveness involved my best friend, Sister Mary, and a teenager accused of murder. When they found the body of five-year-old Lila Ebright in a dumpster, Mary told me "I'm afraid that if I met the murderer I'd want to tear his heart out."

She probably voiced the sentiments of most of Erie, Pennsylvania. For fourteen days the entire city had searched for Lila. She had occupied the front page of the Erie newspapers. All places of business, buses, telephone poles were blanketed with posters of her innocent smiling face. Churches and synagogues had offered special prayers for her safety.

The morning after the child's badly decomposed body was discovered, the phone rang at our convent. My friend, who is the director of our soup kitchen and food pantry, was called to the phone. "Sister Mary, it's me, George. I've got to see you right away."

"The minute I heard his voice I knew it concerned Lila," Mary said. George and his three boys lived across the street from Lila's family. They were two poor families eking out an existence in a tough neighborhood. Minutes after the phone call, Mary was in George's home, trying to be present to a father who had volunteered at the food pantry and whose son was charged with the unimaginable crime. George asked Sister Mary to accompany him to jail that afternoon, "to give my son some spiritual help."

Less than twenty-four hours after she had threatened to rip his heart out, Mary sat facing 17-year-old Scott. That accused murderer was not a faceless stranger, but a boy she knew–a teenager who had accompanied his father to the pantry a few times.

"I needed as much spiritual help as he did," Mary confided. "My heart was full of anger and rage."

"This is difficult for me, Scott," she began. "I don't know what to say to you. If this charge is true, then what you've done is a horrible thing, an act most people find unforgivable." Then Mary told him about the God she believes in and prays to. "My God," she said, "has promised to forgive the most terrible crimes, provided we are sorry. If you killed little Lila, Scott, her family may never forgive you, and maybe they shouldn't. Your family, friends and neighbors might not forgive you, either. God, however, is a different story.

"I don't know how you pray, Scott, but if you did this, then sometime today get down on your knees and beg forgiveness. If you are truly sorry, God will forgive you. Please remember that. Do you understand?" The boy nodded, but stared vacantly ahead.

"I don't believe cheap forgiveness is a solution," Mary said to me later. "Anger in this case is a justifiable emotion, and people like Lila's family and even myself have to work through it. If we lie about the anger and mouth words of easy forgiveness, it only means we will act out the pain in other ways.

"Anyway, it was the best I could do," she stated. "I certainly believe in a God of unlimited forgiveness and compassion, but it was a stark reminder of how far I am from the Scripture: 'Be compassionate as your God is compassionate.'"

Actually, I think she did a good job. Anyway it was not her place to forgive. Only the victim can truly forgive the perpetrator. In this case little Lila is dead and so the family is left to forgive. What to do?

In *Teachings on Love*, Buddhist monk Thich Nhat Hanh recounts a retreat he was leading for U.S. veterans of the Vietnam War. One of the veterans told how almost every one in his platoon had been killed by guerillas. Those who survived were so angry that they baked cookies, put explosives in them and left the cookies on the roadside. When some Vietnamese children saw the cookies they ate them and the explosives went off. The children rolled around the ground in pain until they died in their parents arms. The image of those little ones after the explosives ignited inside their small stomachs was so deeply ingrained on the veteran's heart that, twenty years later, he still could not sit in the same room with children.

Nhat Hanh told him to "begin anew."

"You killed five or six children that day," Nhat Hanh said. "Can you save the lives of five or six children today? You still have your body, you still have your heart; you can do many things to help children who are dying in the present moment."

As horrific as this story is, Nhat Hanh's wisdom is the only possibility for healing that holds hope.

To summarize what I believe about forgiveness: You cannot hurry forgiveness or the anger and pain come back to haunt you. Cheap forgiveness is worthless. Only those who have been wronged have the right to forgive. If you don't forgive wrong done to you, you become, as Stanley Jones noted, like a rattlesnake cornered—you bite and harm yourself. Remember: Begin anew.

You can forgive evil actions but not forget them. Annual observances of the Hiroshima bombing, memorials for the Holocaust, documentaries on apartheid keep us from forgetting and possibly repeating. The danger of remembering is that we hold on to the evil deed or the personal hurt and it paralyzes us, it controls our life. Remember: Begin anew.

Society has the right to punish a wrong, but not to kill the person who committed the evil. It's not enough to say "I'm sorry." Before you can be forgiven you must confess your guilt, resolve not to do it again and make some restitution. Remember: Begin anew.

The most difficult act of forgiveness is to forgive myself. But to forgive without limit means that we must forgive ourselves over and over and over again. Remember: Begin anew.

To forgive without limit is the incarnation of the Divine. Forgiveness is God with us, "mercy within mercy within mercy." God always begins anew.

May my heart forgive without limit.

Reflection/Discussion Questions

1. What thoughts and feelings surfaced during this reading?

2. What is your definition of forgiveness?

3. What is the difference between "cheap forgiveness" and true forgiveness?

4. Is there someone who needs your forgiveness?
   Is there someone from whom you need to ask forgiveness?
   What needs to happen for that forgiveness to take place?

5. Share a time when you were the recipient of "mercy within mercy within mercy."

6. What are your feelings about the author's limits on forgiveness? What are your limits on forgiveness?

7. How does true forgiveness contribute to the development of nonviolence: personally, communally and on a worldwide level?

8. How will you strive to learn how to forgive without measure?

Action Suggestions

1. Pray for the grace to forgive those who have wronged you. Pray for the grace to seek forgiveness from those you have wronged. Journal about your thoughts and feelings.

2. Make a list of those things for which you need to forgive yourself and then say, "I forgive myself for…" Repeat this ritual until you are able to let go and begin anew.

3. Teach others by your example the power of true forgiveness.

May my love for friend, enemy and outcast be without measure.

May my love for friend, enemy and outcast be without measure.

I walked up to an old, old monk and asked him, "What is the audacity of humility?" This man had never met me before, but do you know what his answer was?

"To be the first to say 'I love you.'"

—Tales from the Magic Monastery

A troubled woman came to the Indian saint and sage Ramakrishna, saying, "O Master, I do not find that I love God." And he asked, "Is there nothing, then, that you love?" To this she answered, "My little nephew." And he said to her, "There is your love and service to God, in your love and service to that child."

—Joseph Campbell

Even
after all this time
the sun never says
to the earth,
"You owe Me."

Look
what happens
with a love like that.
It lights up
the whole sky.

—Hafiz

The Nonviolent Moment

May my love for friend, enemy
and outcast be without measure.

One time a beggar woman with cancer of
the face tried to kiss Dorothy Day's hand.
Dorothy commented: "The only thing I
could do was kiss her dirty old face with the
gaping hole in it where an eye and nose
had been. It sounds like a heroic deed, but
it was not. What we avert our eyes from
today can be borne tomorrow when we
have learned a little more about love."

—Source Unknown

In the evening of life we will be judged on love.

—Saint John of the Cross

I was created in love;
therefore nothing can console or liberate me
   save love alone.
The soul is formed of love
   and must ever strive to return to love.
Therefore
it can never find rest nor happiness
   in other things.
It must lose itself in love.

—Mechtild of Magdeburg

The beginning and end of Torah
is performing acts
of loving kindness.

—The Talmud

The Heart of Nonviolence

May my love for friend, enemy
and outcast be without measure.

Reflection/Discussion Questions

1. What thoughts and feelings surfaced during this reading?

2. If today was your Judgment Day and you were judged on the love you shared with your family, friends, strangers, enemies, the world, what do you think God's judgment would be?

3. What is the link between love and nonviolence?

Action Suggestions

1. In your journal, define love. List those who are friend, enemy and outcast.

2. Commit to doing an act of love for persons in each of those categories.

May my needs be few
and my living simple.

May my needs be few and my living simple.

A person who was talking to Gandhi about simple living confessed that he had a greedy mind and couldn't give up his books.'"Then don't give them up," Gandhi told him. "As long as you derive inner help and comfort from anything, you should keep it."

Our life is frittered away by detail.
Simplify, simplify.
—Thoreau

The light of the body is the eye. If therefore thine eye be single, the whole body shall be full of light.
—Jesus

How refreshing,
the whinny of a packhorse
unloaded of everything!
—Zen saying

Sit
Rest
Work.
Alone with yourself,
Never weary.
On the edge of the forest
Live joyfully,
Without desire.
—The Buddha

Those who want the fewest things
are nearest to the gods.
—Socrates

May my needs be few and my living simple.

Among twenty snowy mountains
The only moving thing
Was the eye of the blackbird.
—Wallace Stevens

Consider the lilies of the field,

how they grow;

they toil not,

neither do they spin:

And yet I say unto you,

that even Solomon

in all his glory

was not arrayed

like one of these.

—Jesus

Wealthy patrons invited Ikkyu to a banquet. Ikkyu arrived dressed in his beggar's robes. The host, not recognizing him, chased him away. Ikkyu went home, changed into his ceremonial robe of purple brocade, and returned. With great respect, he was received into the banquet room. There, he put his robe on the cushion saying, "I expect you invited the robe since you turned me away a little while ago," and left.

—Zen story

May my needs be few and my living simple.

Reflection/Discussion Questions

1. What thoughts and feelings surfaced during this reading?

2. What is the difference, for you, between a need and a want?

3. What would a simple lifestyle look like for you?

4. How would it differ from the one you are living now?

5. What about your lifestyle is nonviolent? What is violent?

Action Suggestions

1. Make a list of your possessions. Identify each of them as filling a need or a want.

2. Dialogue with your family/community on what a simple lifestyle would look like for your family/community.

3. Seek information on how over-consumption is violent to others and to our environment. Commit to making the changes necessary so your current lifestyle will begin to become that which you envision.

The Power of Nonviolence

May my actions bear witness
to the suffering of others.

May my actions bear witness to the suffering of others.

The torso of a young man was found in a trash bin, his two legs sawed off. He had been stabbed 10 times–six times in the right side of his face and four times in the upper chest. His legs were found nearby, wrapped in a plastic trash bag.

All murders are shocking. But this one was particularly gruesome, especially for a city like Erie, Pennsylvania, which still prides itself on having a small hometown touch.

Every time a murder occurs in Erie, our sisters gather at the crime site and hold a prayer service. So three days after the body was discovered we joined in song and Scripture at the trash bin near the train station. During the prayer, Sisters Ann and Lynn told us about the visit they had with the victim's father the day before. "We took him a loaf of Sister Irene's bread and he was so touched by this simple gift," Sister Ann said. She talked about how bewildered the father was, wondering why anyone would do such a thing to his son. "We prayed with him and tried to be present to his suffering," she continued. "He was so grateful that we had come bearing bread and words of comfort."

I came to the service feeling numb; this killing was too much for me to stomach. Nothing, I thought, can slow down the escalating violence overtaking our culture. So I was surprised when the tears slid down my face, but I knew what my body was telling me–this was the first time I had really prayed in a long, long time. The sisters who broke bread with the victim's family and the remnant gathered on the street corner were bearing witness. I was bearing witness. And to bear witness is a profound expression of nonviolence. To be present to suffering, just present, without offering answers, is how we most radically follow Jesus' invitation to remember me.

This is the real presence that can lead to healing, to reconciliation, to peace.

I wonder what would happen if all peacemakers thought of actions for justice and peace as bearing witness rather than participating in vigils, rallies, demonstrations, civil disobedience. I wonder if the actions would take on a deeper, more spiritual aura. For example, we are not demonstrating in front of the state prison to abolish the death penalty, we are there to bear witness to the sufferings of both victim and executioner. We are not rallying to change welfare laws, we are in front of the federal building to bear witness to the sufferings of single mothers in minimum-wage jobs. We are getting arrested because a newer nuclear weapon is added to the arsenal, we are at the White House to bear witness to the sufferings of butchered boy soldiers of the armies, of women raped in war, of innocent children wounded and slain.

If our stance in right action was immersion in the suffering of others, rather than trying to fix injustice, would the circle of compassion widen?

Bernie Glassman, Zen abbot, author and founder of a network of businesses that employ the poor in Yonkers, started a new religious order whose charism is bearing witness. You might find members of the Zen Peacemaker Order sitting in prayer from sunrise to sunset at Auschwitz, bearing witness. Or in a drug-infested, gang-controlled neighborhood in the Bronx, bearing witness. The Zen Peacemaking Order believes that peace comes when we lead a questioning life, a life of unknowing, without fixed ideas or answers. Peace comes when we are open enough to bear witness to all of life, both its joys and sufferings. Peace comes by being awake, present and open to every unfolding moment, to all of reality. Peace comes not by having answers or passing judgment on those with whom we disagree, but by bearing witness to the diversity and oneness of all living beings. Out of that process of bearing witness, the right action of making peace, of healing, arises. In the introduction to *Bearing Witness: A Zen Master's Lessons in Making Peace*, Glassman writes:

"Every creature, every person, every phenomenon is just another aspect of who we are. A little girl, a mother, a killer, a policeman are all aspects of who we are. So is the nightingale, the hawk that kills the nightingale, and the hunter who kills the hawk. We are all victims, the perpetrators, and the people who stand indifferently by. We are the feelings and thoughts of all these people, who are nothing other than aspects of ourselves. We are not attracted or repelled, for we are them.

"The Buddhist service that we perform on the streets of New York City's Bowery begins: 'Attention! Attention!' when we say 'Attention!' what do we mean? When we really listen, when we really pay attention to the sounds of joy and suffering in the universe, then we are not separate from them, we become them. Because in reality we are not separate from those who suffer. We are them; they are us. And once we listen, we have to act. The functioning that comes out of listening–out of 'Attention!'–is compassionate action. If we don't listen, we can't act with compassion."

Two stories dramatize what Glassman is talking about. The first is told about Taigu Ryokan, the Japanese Zen monk and poet (1759-1831). Ryokan was asked by his brother to visit his house and speak to his delinquent son. Ryokan came and did not say a word of admonition to the boy. He stayed overnight and prepared to leave the next morning. As the wayward nephew was lacing up Ryokan's sandals, he felt a drop of warm water. Glancing up, he saw Ryokan looking down at him, his eyes full of tears. Ryokan then returned home, and the nephew changed for the better.

The one warm tear of Ryokan is enough. Ryokan does not say a word but becomes one with the nephew. Ryokan's tear bears witness to the inner pain and suffering of his nephew. The nephew knows he is loved. And any meaningful change, any genuine change of heart, can only happen when the one in error feels truly loved. In this story, Ryokan's nephew changes for the better. But Ryokan changes, too. He becomes softer, more sensitive to the cries of the world; his tear is evidence of that. It doesn't always happen that neatly but I believe that bearing witness to the suffering of others rather than screaming out their sins does, in the long run, enable compassion to erupt like fields of wildflowers, uncontainable beauty that spreads and springs up where you least expect. And this is the foundation of healing and peace.

The second story is a Zen koan. It goes like this: One day Chau-Chou fell down in the snow and called out, "Help me up; help me up." A monk came and lay down beside him. Then Chau-Chou got up and went away.

The monk bears witness to Chau-Chou's suffering by

presence. He doesn't try to advise or assist Chau-Chou, the victim. He does not judge him for staying immobile in the snow, or ask him how it happened. He merely lies next to Chau-Chou and the monk's compassionate presence is enough. Chau-Chou is empowered to lift himself out of the cold and continue his journey.

Bearing witness calls for humility. None of us can enter fully into the suffering of another and certainly we can't bear witness to all suffering. But we can widen our circle of compassion beyond ourselves and risk the unknown, trusting that the right action will arise. All his life Gandhi explored peacemaking through nonviolence and called his autobiography *My Experiments with Truth*. Maybe peacemakers today could look at their efforts of nonviolence as *My Experiments with Bearing Witness*.

May my actions bear witness to the suffering of others.

Reflection/Discussion Questions

1. What thoughts and feelings surfaced during this reading?

2. How do you respond to Jesus' invitation to "remember me"?

3. What does "bearing witness" mean to you?
   Do you see it as different from participating in actions for justice and peace?
   Why or why not?

4. Bernie Glassman, in *Bearing Witness: A Zen Master's Lessons in Making Peace*, writes that "A ittle girl, a mother, a killer, a policeman are all aspects of who we are."
   Do you agree or disagree? Why?

5. Define nonviolence as it relates to action and to bearing witness.
   Is there a difference?
   Why or why not?

6. What would your life look like if you committed to living a life of unknowing—open to all life offers, joy and suffering?

Action Suggestions

1. Read *Bearing Witness: A Zen Master's Lessons in Making Peace* by Bernie Glassman.

2. Enter into another's pain—be present to comfort, not to fix.

3. Consciously pay attention and bear witness at the next vigil/ action. Journal about how it felt. What, if anything, was different?

May my hands
never harm a living being.

May my hands never harm a living being.

What's this little brown insect
walking
    zigzag
across the sunny white page
of Su Tung-po's poem?

Fly away, tiny mite,
even your life is tender—
I lift the book and blow you
into the dazzling void.

—Allen Ginsberg

Don't
kill
him!
the fly
it wrings its hands,
its feet.

—Issa

Imagine that you are creating a fabric of
human destiny with the object of making
men and women happy in the end…but
that it is essential and inevitable to torture
to death only one tiny creature…and to
found that edifice on its unavenged tears:
would you consent to be the architect on
those conditions? Tell me, and tell me
the truth?

—Feodor Dostoyevsky

May my hands never harm a living being.

"Pardon me,"
said the monkey
as he placed the protesting fish
on the branch of a tree,
"I am only saving you from drowning."
—Told by Anthony De Mello

The eyes of the saint
    make all beauty holy
and the hands of the saint
    consecrate everything they touch
    to the glory of God,
and the saint is never offended by anything
    and judges no one's sin
    because the saint does not know sin.
The saint knows the mercy of God.
—Thomas Merton

May my hands never harm a living being.

Reflection/Discussion Questions

1. What thoughts and feelings surfaced during these readings?

2. What reading disturbed you the most?
   Why?

3. How would you respond to Walt Whitman's piece?
   To Dostoyevsky's?

4. What does Anthony De Mello's piece say to you?

5. What "living beings" do you not consider sacred and deserving of life?

6. What images of God have your hands harmed this past week?

Action Suggestions

1. Copy one of the readings and place it where you will read it daily.

2. Commit to treating all living creatures as sacred and deserving of life, one day at a time. Journal about your thoughts and feelings. Was your day different? How and why?

*May my steps stay
on the journey of justice.*

May my steps stay on the journey of justice.

Some things you must always be unable to bear. Some things you must never stop refusing to bear. Injustice and outrage and dishonor and shame. No matter how young you are or how old you have got. Not for kudos and not for cash, your picture in the paper nor money in the bank, neither. Just refuse to bear them.

—**William Faulkner**

"When will justice come to Athens?"
they asked Thucydides.
And he answered,
"Justice will not come to Athens
until those who are not injured
are as indignant as those who are."

Keep the flame going,
but low; burning,
but not burning up.
—**Daniel Berrigan**

In the face of suffering, one has no right to turn away, not to see. In the face of injustice, one may not look the other way. When someone suffers, and it is not you, they come first. Their suffering gives them priority. ...To watch over another who grieves is a more urgent duty than to think of God.

—**Elie Wiesel**

What is a religious person? "A religious person," Rabbi Heschel would say, "is someone who suffers the harm done to other people."

The Nonviolent Moment

May my steps stay on the journey of justice.

Sandinista Avioncitos

The little airplanes of the heart
with their brave little propellers
What can they do
against the winds of darkness
even as butterflies
are beaten back by hurricanes
yet do not die
They lie in wait wherever
they can hide and hang
their fine wings folded
and when the killer-wind dies
they flutter forth again
into the new-blown light
live as leaves

—Lawrence Ferlinghetti

_There may be times when we are powerless to prevent injustice,
but there must never be a time when we fail to protest._

—Elie Wiesel

Whenever you are in doubt, as when the
self becomes too much with you, try the
following experiment. Recall the face of the
poorest and most helpless person you have
ever seen and ask yourself if the step you
contemplate is going to be of any use to
that person...then you will find your doubts
and your self melting away.

—Gandhi

May my steps stay on the journey of justice.

Reflection/Discussion Questions

1. What thoughts and feelings surfaced during these readings?

2. How does "bearing witness" relate to righteous anger?

3 Share where you see yourself on the journey of justice.

4. What injustices do you refuse to bear?
   How do you stand against them?

5. What injustices are difficult for you to stand against?

6. What commitment are you making to a future you will not see?

Action Suggestions

1. Choose an injustice in your neighborhood and take a stand against it.

2. Choose an injustice in your country and take a stand against it.

3. Choose an injustice in the world and take a stand against it.

4. Meditate daily on the words of Elie Wiesel, journal about your thoughts and feelings and then act on what the journey of justice demands of you.

The Courage
of Nonviolence

*May my tongue speak for the poor
without fear of the powerful.*

May my tongue speak for the poor
without fear of the powerful.

"The spirit of boldness and courage makes all other virtues possible," Winston Churchill said. Jesus certainly knew this because he addressed the issue of fear over and over again. In the Gospel of Luke, for example, the angels tell Zechariah and Mary and the shepherds to "fear not" (Lk. 1:13, 30; 2:10). "Do not be afraid," are the first words that Jesus says to Simon Peter (Lk. 5:10). He tells the crowd gathered around Jarius that "fear is useless" (Lk. 8:50). He addresses us tenderly with "fear not little flock" (Lk. 12:32).

Even on Resurrection Sunday the Scriptures try to teach us that before any "good news" can be given to the poor, fear must be overcome. Easter evening finds the disciples huddled together behind closed doors because they were afraid of the religious leaders who had put Jesus to death.

No one had locked the disciples in the upper room; they had turned the key themselves. They had shut themselves in a prison of their own making. The apostles are frightened of being alone and leaderless. They are frightened of the personal demons unleashed in the past few days—betrayal, cowardice. They are frightened of the authorities, both religious and secular, who have power over life and death. They are frightened of the cross and empty tomb. And fear has paralyzed them.

I experienced such traumatic fear in December 1983 when I was part of a group of 150 churchwomen who were going on a peace pilgrimage to Honduras. Our plan was to pray for peace in that troubled region at naval and air bases and at the headquarters of the contras, the right-wing Nicaraguan paramilitary. Before departing for Tegucigalpa we had a day and a half orientation session in Miami. The delegation was good-hearted and committed, but terribly inexperienced. For the majority, this was their first major nonviolent direct action. Most had no training or background in street nonviolence. And here we were, planning to hike into the mountains alone and pray in front of contra strongholds. For the first time in my life, I experienced blood-freezing fear. All I could imagine was sheep being led to the slaughter.

I didn't sleep for two nights. I tried to meditate, to calm myself by reciting my favorite prayer: "Let nothing disturb thee, let nothing frighten thee. All things are changing. God alone is changeless. Patience attains the goal. One who has God lacks nothing. God alone fills all our needs." But to no use. I was filled with fear–deep, deep fear. The poor of Honduras and Nicaragua were forgotten. I was afraid to act on their behalf because I feared the powerful. The powerful could kill me and I was afraid to die.

Whether the cause of my fear was real, exaggerated or imaginary doesn't matter. What counts is that for me, I came face-to-face with the cost of discipleship and recoiled from the cross.

Relief, not anger, was what I felt when the Honduran military surrounded our plane with tanks on the runway of the Tegucigalpa airport, boarded it, and told us we were not welcome there. I said a prayer of thanksgiving, instead of a prayer for renewed courage, when the plane flew back to Miami.

That night NBC was showing–of all things–*Choices of the Heart,* a movie based on the life of Jean Donovan, one of the four U.S. missionaries raped and murdered in El Salvador in 1980. We didn't get back to our rooms until late that evening so I only caught the end of the movie. It was enough. In one of the final scenes, Jean Donovan is talking about her friend, Sister Ita Ford, one of the other women who was murdered. She was recounting how Ita had almost drowned a few months before her brutal murder. During a flash flood Ita and another sister drove off the road and into a river. Ita told Jean how she felt herself drowning, trapped in the car under water. "I didn't even struggle," she told Jean. "I felt myself going under and said, 'Receive me, God, I'm ready.'"

I listened to Ita's words all night long: "Receive me, God, I'm ready." Amazing. What must it be like to know the presence of God with such certainty. To have God so near that death loses its sting.

Martin Luther King, Jr. knew this presence. He found it in the midst of the Civil Rights struggle. One night, when he was in bed about to fall asleep, the phone rang. A voice on the other end said, "Listen, nigger, we've taken all we want from you. Before next week, you'll be sorry you ever came to Montgomery." Dr. King hung up and suddenly all his fears came crashing down on him. He got up and heated a pot of coffee. Then he sat down at the kitchen table, bowed his head and prayed: "People are looking to me for leadership, and if I stand before them without

May my tongue speak for the poor
without fear of the powerful.

strength and courage, they too will falter. I am at the end of my powers. I have nothing left. I've come to the point where I can't face it alone." At that moment Dr. King said he felt the personal presence of God in his life as he had never felt it before. All his fears disappeared and his strength and courage returned. From that time on he never wavered in his pursuit of justice, even though it cost him much personal anguish and eventually his life.

Jean Goss-Myer, one of the founders of the Fellowship of Reconciliation, had a similar experience. Jean, who had been imprisoned and tortured in Brazil for working with Christian base communities, was asked in an interview whether he had experienced great fear in jail.

Jean said, "I'm afraid of suffering. I can't stand heroism. That's how I am. And yet I've been a prisoner, been tortured and humiliated. How could I have lived through all that? Yet I can assure you that since my meeting with Christ, I have never been afraid. I've been worried, but I have never really been afraid anymore. I know I could face up to the whole world. I am absolutely certain that Christ loves us more than we can dream, think, know or believe, that he loves us beyond all our faults. That sort of faith wipes away every fear. The first time I was tortured was in 1942. Soldiers took me from the prison camp to a fortress nine kilometers away. I was handcuffed and I was praying–and I was overwhelmed with joy. It was extraordinary...."

The closest I've come to experiencing this presence and joy was on the second anniversary of the death of the four women martyred in El Salvador.

May my tongue speak for the poor
without fear of the powerful.

I was one of twelve women who went to Washington in 1982 to pray in the U.S. Capitol that our government would convert from works of war by ceasing military aid to Central America.

The police cleared the rotunda of supporters and tourists, and the twelve of us knelt in a circle praying aloud, feeling rather alone and powerless in the huge foyer, surrounded by Secret Service and police. Then a powerful thing happened. We started singing.

We celebrated the lives of Ita Ford, Maura Clarke, Dorothy Kazel and Jean Donovan by singing God's praises until we thought our hearts would break.

For a brief moment I knew how the early Christians could walk into the Colliseum, into the jaws of lions, singing. I felt lifted up, bonded forever to the four women martyrs of El Salvador, united with all who suffered and shed blood for justice and human rights. There was nothing to fear, ever. God's truth and justice would prevail.

The officer in charge approached each of us individually, read us our rights and gave a final warning—unless we left the rotunda immediately we would be arrested. It was with great freedom that each of us could smile softly, look the officer in the eye and sing: "We proclaim the greatness of God...for God hears the cry of the poor."

That day I was blessed with an insight into the communion of saints. And the power of the human spirit, mortal and frail though it be, never seemed so indestructible.

One more thing about facing fears. The fear that Jesus confronted in the Gospels is fear of religious authorities. Jesus confronts the system that claims it speaks for God.

The Nonviolent Moment

May my tongue speak for the poor
without fear of the powerful.

He called into question the Sabbath laws, the taboo against women, the stoning of prostitutes, the demonizing of lepers, tax collectors and Samaritans.

For me, it has always been easier to resist the state, to demonstrate against its systemic injustice, its lust for violence. In October 1979 when Pope John Paul II addressed women religious at the Shrine of the Immaculate Conception in Washington, D.C., I was one of about two dozen sisters, wearing blue arm bands, who were to stand when he spoke–in protest over the treatment of women in the church. Sister of Mercy Therese Kane, head of the Leadership Conference of Women Religious at the time, addressed the congregation prior to the Pope's presentation. She gave a strong, pointed address, calling for equality in the church. I remember leaning over to the sister next to me and saying, "We don't have to stand now. She said everything for us." I will be forever grateful that my sister Benedictine yanked me by the arm and said, "Get on your feet." I was shaking more than I ever did when getting arrested in front of the White House or being handcuffed and thrown in a paddy wagon.

Rightfully, I get more of my self-identity from being a member of the Catholic Church than from being a citizen of the United States. The church is my family so dissent is difficult. And yet...it is Jesus who lashed out at the hypocrisy of religious leaders and Jesus who broke unjust religious laws with abandon. It is Jesus who reminds us that when religion places unbearable burdens on people, the yoke must be lifted. It is Jesus who died at the hands of religious authorities.

May my tongue speak for the poor
without fear of the powerful.

"Those who would give light must endure burning," a political prisoner wrote. Followers of Jesus might well consider what light is needed in the church today. What intensity of burning are we willing to endure to raise questions regarding gay and lesbian issues and women serving as ordained ministers in the Roman Catholic Church? What boldness and courage is needed from us so that justice in our church becomes possible?

May my tongue speak for the poor
without fear of the powerful.

Reflection/Discussion Questions

1. What thoughts and feelings surfaced during this reading?

2. Of what and whom are you afraid?

3. Are you in a prison of your own making? Describe it.

4. Share a moment when you were paralyzed by fear and were unable to overcome it.
   What hindered you?

5. Can you identify with the struggle the people in this reading faced?
   Can you identify with the feeling of having your fears disappear after praying?

6. Who has helped you to "stand up" when you have been fearful?

Action Suggestions

1. Name the fears that prevent you from speaking truth to power for the voiceless. Pray daily to be released from your fears and commit to acting to overcome them.

2. Share your fears, struggles and successes with others who may need support as they struggle with their fears.

The Nonviolent Moment

May my prayers rise
with patient discontent
until no child is hungry.

May my prayers rise with patient discontent
until no child is hungry.

I will set my face to the wind and scatter my handful of seeds. It is no big thing to scatter seeds, but I must have the courage to keep facing the wind.
—**Arabic proverb**

The feeding of those that are hungry
is a form of contemplation.
—**Simone Weil**

The satiated person and the hungry
one do not see the same thing when
they look upon a loaf of bread.
—**Rumi**

The older I get the more I feel that faithfulness and perseverance are the greatest of virtues—accepting the sense of failure we all must have in our work, in the work of others around us, since Christ was the world's greatest failure.
—**Dorothy Day**

Life only demands from you
the strength you possess.
Only one feat is possible—
not to have run away.
—**Dag Hammarskjold**

A rabbi, upon entering a room in his home, saw his son deep in prayer. In the corner stood a cradle with a crying baby. The rabbi asked his son, "Can't you hear? There's a baby crying in this room." The son said, "Father, I was lost in God." And the rabbi said, "One who is lost in God can see the very fly crawling up the wall."
—**Abel Herzberg**

May my prayers rise with patient discontent
until no child is hungry.

Whenever I'm feeling discouraged
I vow with all beings
to remember how Ling-yun
saw peach trees bloom
after thirty long years.
—Robert Aitken Roshi

One day a boy was watching a holy man praying on the banks of a river in India. When the holy man completed his prayer, the boy went over and asked him, "Will you teach me to pray?"

The holy man studied the boy's face carefully. Then he gripped the boy's head in his hands and plunged it forcefully into the water. The boy struggled frantically, trying to free himself in order to breathe. Finally, the holy man released his hold.

When the boy was able to get his breath, he gasped, "What did you do that for?"

The holy man said, "I just gave you the first lesson."

"What do you mean?" asked the astonished boy.

"Well," said the holy man, "when you long to pray as much as you longed to breathe when your head was under water—only then will I be able to teach you to pray."

—Source Unknown

Feeding the hungry
is a greater work
than raising the dead.
—St. John Chrysostom

The world is filled
with churchgoers
and the world is filled
with the obscenely poor.
Go figure.
—Joan D. Chittister, OSB

May my prayers rise with patient discontent
until no child is hungry.

Reflection/Discussion Questions

1. What thoughts and feelings surfaced during these readings?

2. Feeding the hungry is one of the corporal works of mercy.
   Are you feeding the hungry?
   Is there more you could be doing?
   What will you do and when will you begin?

3. Can you identify with the words of Dorothy Day?
   Where do you need to practice the virtues of faithfulness and perseverance?

4. What quote challenged you the most and why?

5. What do the words "patient discontent" mean to you?

6. Share a time when you felt you were truly hungry.

Action Suggestions

1. Using a picture of hungry children, meditate each day, praying for God's guidance to help you do your part in changing that picture.

2. Join an organization whose primary focus is to feed the hungry—an organization such as Bread for the World.

3. Volunteer at a soup kitchen.

4. Carry a cooler in your car with some bag lunches and give them to those who have been reduced to begging for food.

5. Tap a percentage of your grocery bill and donate it to an organization that feeds the hungry.

The Grace of Nonviolence

*May my life's work be a passion
for peace and nonviolence.*

May my life's work be a passion for peace and nonviolence.

One night a moth sees a lamp, a burning flame
enclosed in glass. It spends the whole night bump-
ing against the glass, trying to become one with the
flame. In the morning it returns to its friends and tells
them of the beautiful thing it has seen. They say,
"You don't look the better for it." So it goes back the
next night and somehow or other, gets through.
For an eternal instant it achieves its goal:
it becomes the flame
—"Thou art that."

—Hallaj

Do not seek illumination
unless you seek it
as a man whose hair is on fire
seeks a pond.
—Sri Ramakrishna

Abba Lot went to see Abba Joseph and said, "Abba, as much as
I am able I practice a small rule, all the little fasts, some prayer and
meditation, and remain quiet, and as much as possible I keep my
thoughts clean. What else should I do?" Then the old man stood
up and stretched out his hands toward heaven, and his fingers
became like the torches of flame. And he said, "Why not be turned
into fire?"

—From the *Desert Fathers and Mothers*

May my life's work be a passion for peace and nonviolence.

The flaw in the new militants is that in their passion to live in a more human world they sometimes fail to relish those first fruits that are present today. They lack a festive clan. Earnest, committed, and even zealous, they often suffer from a fatal humorlessness. Their "no" is much louder than their "yes" and they seem to skirt very close to the borders of nihilism.

—Harvey Cox

STARWISH
The stars
Shine
Like silver
In the sky
When it is
Dark.
They guard
My bed.
They make
Animals
Or humans
Like dot
To dot.
I wish
On certain
Stars.
Will they come true some day?
—Patrick Bruno, 9

May my life's work be a passion for peace and nonviolence.

Reflection/Discussion Questions

1. What thoughts and feelings surfaced during these readings?

2. What does the word "passion" mean to you?

3. What do you say is your life's work?
   What would others say?

4. Have you felt the kind of passion described in the readings?
   When?

5. What are you passionate about?

6. Are you passionate about working to make visible the
   Kingdom of God?

Action Suggestions

1. Pray daily for grace and seek to develop a passion for
   peace and nonviolence.

2. Read about the practitioners of nonviolence and how they
   lived their lives.

3. Examine your life. Are you pouring your energies into
   something lasting?
   If not, what changes need to be made?
   Commit to begin making those changes.

4. Examine what you are doing to make visible the Kingdom.
   What more can you do?
   Begin to act within your family, your community, your work
   environment, your country and the world in ways that will
   bring about peace and nonviolence.

May my soul rejoice
in the present moment.

May my soul rejoice in the present moment.

A Zen saying reads: "When you walk, just walk; when sitting; just sit. Above all don't wobble." I translate that to mean "Be Present." When you eat, don't think about the letter you have to write but concentrate on the grapefruit slice in your mouth. When you listen to music, don't think of the cup of coffee you want to drink but be mindful of the melody.

In the 70s I was introduced to the idea of "mindfulness," of being present to the moment, through the writings of Thich Nhat Hanh, the Buddhist monk. In *The Miracle of Being Awake,* Nhat Hanh wrote that if we cannot "wash the dishes to wash the dishes...we are completely incapable of realizing the miracle of life while standing at the sink...we are incapable of actually living one minute of life."

Nhat Hanh's words sent me reeling. Have I ever actually lived one minute of life? Really eaten an apple, dusted a chair, looked at another human being?

Well...on occasion. But most of the time my mind flitters on the past or flies to the future instead of being fully alive to the present moment.

What an embarrassing admission for someone living in a monastery. After all, monasteries exist to foster mindfulness. To nurture concentration, novices in some monasteries spend months learning how to pour a cup of tea, how to close a door.

In Japan, for example, one order of monks tries to develop mindfulness, a sense of the sacred, in its novices

The Nonviolent Moment

by having them spend their training period always walking with a broom, sweeping the ground in front of them to avoid killing any insects.

The intent of this monastic training is awareness or mindfulness or contemplation. The hope is that you begin to see creation as it really is: sacred. The hope is that you begin to see yourself as you really are: sacred. Or as one writer said: "Concentration becomes, finally, consecration."

In contemplation–in the kiss of God–my sense of the sacred is awakened and the dichotomy between all created things and creator dissolves. I begin to see all creation as sacrament, as visible sign of invisible divine presence. I see all creation as good, as sharing in the source of goodness that created it.

If I see like this, then any hatred or fear or abhorrence or misuse of created things is akin to blasphemy: an insult, a show of contempt, a lack of reverence for God. To be aware of the world as Hopkins was, "charged with the grandeur of God," makes it impossible for a seeker to fill the earth with any tint of ugliness, or cheapness, or cynicism or despair. To awaken is to look on any human face and be moved to create a world where such beauty is honored and given a chance for a decent life.

But how can I learn to see that God who is beyond all things and yet in all things, even the most infinitesimal particle? How can I nurture a sense of reverence, wonder, and sacredness in the face of mass consumerism, waste, pollution and the synthetic?

Saint Benedict gives us a hint. "Treat all goods as sacred vessels of the altar," he writes. And Dostoyevsky echoes, "Love all God's creation, the whole and every grain of sand in it. Love every leaf, every ray of God's light. Love the plants, love everything. If you love everything, you will perceive the divine mystery of all things. Once you perceive it, you will begin to comprehend it better every day. And you will come at last to love the whole world with an all-embracing love."

You become mindful, in other words, by practicing mindfulness. With such an attitude it becomes impossible to pollute the earth, to waste scarce resources, to use more than I need, to be dispassionate and uncaring about all life issues.

Through the centuries, the saints have recommended certain practices to help arrive at this awareness of the divine within. Meditation, prayer, silence, fasting, repetition of holy words, reflective reading of scriptures can lead to contemplation, to a "long, loving look at the real."

The Quaker mystic Thomas Kelly wrote about people like this, people so immersed in the Heart of God, people so aflame with God's love that "creation has a new value...wherein not a sparrow falls to the ground without the Father." Kelly asked, "Have you experienced this concern for the sparrow's fall?" I mulled the question, Mary Lou, have you ever experienced concern for the sparrow's fall? And I had to reply, "No." I am not yet "awake"; the sparrow is not yet precious in my sight.

And if I am not mindful of the sparrow, will I be mindful of the hungry child in Ethiopia, the convicted murderer on death row, the abused woman next door, the dying children of Iraq?

Kelly continues his description of the contemplative, the person fully awake: "There is a tendering of the soul toward everything in creation, from the sparrow's fall to the slave under the lash...there is a sense in which, in its terrible tenderness, we become one with God."

Enlightenment, then, is awakening to the reality that at every moment I am in God and God is in me. This is a reality, of course, whether I recognize it or not. The fact is that if God were separate from me, I would cease to be. God, as Thmas Merton kept reminding us, is the hidden ground of all that exists, the hidden ground of love. Everyone, I believe, is given the grace of awakening. Sometimes the awakening comes with the force of a great wind, sometimes in a whisper.

One of my awakening experiences happened in the Metropolitan Museum of Art in New York City in 1978 when I walked into the room where the Angel Tree is shown every Christmas. It was my first visit there and I had no idea where I was going, so I just followed a large crowd of bustling shoppers and tourists into a large room. Immediately the talking and bustling stopped and a great silence filled the space. In front of me was a thirty-foot blue spruce, covered with elegant hand-sculptured angels. How to describe them? How to capture the beauty and the radiance of their faces, bathed in soft tree lights? The fifty or so angels seemed in flight, their hair waving wildly. Many were swinging silver-gilt censors; some were just poised in adoration. All were turned toward the tiny child in the crib. Under the tree were two hundred figurines: magi, shepherds, animals, townspeople and travelers, representatives from every corner of the earth, all hurrying towards the manger.

But it was the angels that captured me—their faces aglow with awe and wonder and mystery. And then in this hushed hall, "O Holy Night" poured out of the loudspeakers and bathed the crowd in the sacred. All I wanted to do was prostrate and adore.

Psychologists call such moments "peak experiences," spiritual writers refer to them as "contemplative moments," poets speak of "spiritual wonder." Whatever you attempt to label the experience, I was given the grace to lose myself and yet be truly present, acutely aware of my surroundings and in union with all that is.

Sometimes these intense moments of awareness are given to us because we need them to get through difficulties or through periods of darkness or dry times. Sometimes they are given to us as stepping-stones, hinge points in our spiritual journeys. Whatever the reason, they are pure gift.

But any good spiritual teacher will warn against looking for God only in the extraordinary. Core experiences, mystical moments, we must let them come and go. The result of genuine spiritual training is to arrive at the day when we can see the sacred in the simple, the extraordinary in the ordinary. We forget all too easily the incarnation, that God is found in the stuff of human life.

In his book, *A Journey to Ladakh*, Andrew Harvey recorded one of the most profound stories of awakening that I've come across in my lifetime. On pilgrimage in the mountainous terrain of northern India, Harvey visited monastery after monastery, participating with great zeal in all Buddhist rituals. So afire was he with the desire for enlightenment that he was almost blinded by a passion to possess the ultimate experience.

One day as he walked toward a remote monastery he noticed the dance of the sun on the stone path. "I have no choice," he wrote, "but to be alive to this landscape and this light." He spent the afternoon being present to the beauty of light on rocks, the stream by the path, the apricot trees that dotted the stark landscape and concluded that such presence "is enough."

He never arrived at the monastery that afternoon, but he did have his moment of enlightenment. And here was his marvelous insight: that the striking beauty of the Land of the Snows was not dependent upon him nor did it care about his existence–it was just there. In fact it had been there for millenniums and would remain there beyond his brief breath of a life. He was insignificant to the grandeur of creation and to the cycle of the ages.

He wrote, "The things that ignore us save us in the end. Their presence awakens silence in us; they refresh our courage with the purity of their detachment."

Those two insights: just to be present to the moment "is enough" and "the things that ignore us save us in the end" are all I need to contemplate the rest of my life.

Let us awaken. And with grateful hearts join Rumi, the Sufi poet and mystic, in proclaiming:

The law of wonder rules
my life at last. In each
leaping second I live afresh.

May my soul rejoice in the present moment.

Reflection/Discussion Questions

1. What thoughts and feelings surfaced during this reading?

2. When was the last time you were present to the moment, when you were actually living one minute of life?

3. Have you met someone who has this quality of mindfulness/ contemplation?
   Share the experience. How did the encounter make you feel?

4. When, if ever, have you been aware that the world was "charged with the grandeur of God"?

5. Share a "peak experience." Share a moment when you saw God in the ordinary.

6. Who or what are you not mindful of?

Action Suggestions

1. Commit to developing the gift of being present. Choose daily one or more actions when you will be mindful of what you are doing. Journal about your thoughts and feelings.

2. Seek to see the divine in yourself and in all creation. Ask for the grace to love everything.

3. Commit to being mindful of the sacredness of all creation and act accordingly.

The Nonviolent Moment

The Soul of Nonviolence

*May my imagination
overcome death and despair
with new possibility.*

*May my imagination overcome death and despair
with new possibility.*

Recently I visited the John Lennon exhibit at the Rock and Roll Hall of Fame in Cleveland, Ohio. A very moving tribute with a documentary on John, walls of framed lyrics in handwriting, original drawings and displays of personal memorabilia including Yoko and John's bed made out of two church pews and the brown bag containing all John's belongings the night he was gunned down. Over the loudspeakers, John sings to us– "All we are saying is give peace a chance," "Beautiful Boy," and "Imagine," my all-time favorite.

It's a moving tribute to a creative genius and a testimony to his pursuit of peace and love and imagination. There is a wishing tree at the exhibit. Guests are asked to write a wish and hang it on the tree. "I wish we would give peace a chance, John." "I wish our government had your imagination, John." "I wish you were still here, John, and could talk to my father. He loves you so." And then this one, swinging loosely from a branch, "I wish Yoko Ono was dead."

It stopped me cold, ripped the joy from an afternoon spent with hope. How? How can someone finish walking through three floors of a tribute to human possibility and end up with hate? When the security guard wasn't looking, I grabbed that slip of paper from the tree and slipped it into my pocket. Enough. Blame me for censorship if you want, but I will no longer expose children to messages of despair and hate. It's the least I could do for John Lennon.

May my imagination overcome death and despair
with new possibility.

It's the least I could do to pay tribute to imagination and possibility.

Once I heard a taped interview with John Lennon on the radio, a section of which I copied into my journal. Lennon was asked why he devoted so much energy to peace and wasn't that a waste of time. Lennon replied that he believed it was Leonardo DaVinci who made flying possible by projecting it, by bringing it into people's consciousness as even a possibility. "What a person projects will eventually happen," Lennon said. "Therefore I always want to project peace. I want to put the possibility of peace into the public imagination. And I know, as certain as I am standing here," Lennon told the interviewer, "I know that someday peace will be."

Can we imagine peace and nonviolence? Can we imagine what ear has not heard, what eye has not seen, what has not yet captured the human heart? In his landmark book, *The Prophetic Imagination*, Walter Brueggemann writes: "The church must be a poetic community. A poetic community that offers explosive, concrete, subversive, critical images around which people can reorganize their lives."

We are desperate for poetry, for that which surprises and liberates us, opens our minds to new possibilities, poetry that nurtures hope beyond cynicism, that frees us and evokes a new social reality.

I think of people like Victor Jara, most beloved poet and folk singer of Chile. On the day that President Allende was overthrown in the U.S.-backed coup, Jara and 5,000 other Allende sympathizers were herded into Chile's National Stadium. It is said that Jara played his guitar and sang songs of freedom and hope while the military interrogated and tortured, raped the women and killed hundreds of his friends. And that he kept singing when they cut off his fingers one by one, broke his back and shot him. His song:

> *Now I want to live*
> *Beside my son and brother*
> *Going on to construct the springtime*
> *On which we all work every day.*
> *You can't scare me with threats*
> *You masters of misery.*
> *The star of hope*
> *Continues to be ours.*

Jara's imagination overcame death and despair with new possibility.

Or I think of storytellers like Eduardo Galeano. He tells us that in Uruguay political prisoners may not talk without permission, or whistle, smile, sing, walk fast, or greet other prisoners, nor may they receive drawings of pregnant women, couples, butterflies or birds.

A schoolteacher is jailed "for having ideological ideas" and undergoes torture. One day, the story goes, the schoolteacher is visited by his daughter, Milay, age 5. She brings him a drawing of birds. The guards grab the paper and destroy it at the entrance of the jail.

On the following Sunday, Milay brings him a drawing of trees. Trees are not forbidden, and the drawing gets through. The schoolteacher praises her work and asks

May my imagination overcome death and despair with new possibility.

about the colored circles scattered in the treetops, many small circles half-hidden among the branches: "Are they oranges? What fruit is it?" Little Milay puts her finger to her mouth: "Shh." And she whispers in his ear, "Silly, don't you see they're eyes? They're the eyes of the birds that I've smuggled in for you."

The storyteller Galeano and little Milay overcome death and despair with new possibility.

I think of people like the poet Robert Desnos, who, on his way to the ovens in Buchenwald, grabbed the hands of his fellow Jews who were on the truck and began to read their palms. "I see a long life line in this palm," he said aloud. "I see a happy marriage and three children," he said to another. "I see wealth and prosperity," he said to a third. Soon the entire truckload of condemned men came alive with rising hope and were thrusting their hands at him. "Read mine. Read mine," they shouted. The excitement for life, the hope of tomorrow so confused the Nazi soldiers that they turned the truck around and went back to camp.

Desnos, the poet, overcame death and despair with new possibility.

And I think of people like Gene Knudsen Hoffman who lives in Santa Barbara and for 20 years has been speaking and writing about "compassionate listening." She goes into troubled spots like the Middle East and brings together those on both sides of the conflict. "We peace people have always listened to the oppressed and disenfranchised," she writes. "That's very important. One of the new steps I think we should take is to listen to those we

May my imagination overcome death and despair
with new possibility.

consider 'the enemy,' with the same openness, nonjudg-
ment, and compassion we bring to those with whom our
sympathies lie. Everyone has a partial truth, and we must
listen, discern, acknowledge this partial truth in everyone–particularly those with whom we disagree. We must
learn to listen deeply and understand the suffering of both
sides." And I think of Nelson Mandela and Bishop Tutu
who led South Africa toward healing through the Truth
and Reconciliation Commissions. Or we can turn to Aus-
tralia where, in 1988, the people created "Sorry Days" and
apologized to the indigenous people for the crime their
government committed in stealing aborigines' children. All
of these give us glimpses of a new heaven and a new Earth.

But most of all I think of Jesus. Through stories and
parable and a brief life that lit a black sky with a moment
of brilliant light, Jesus helped us to imagine. His words
and life were a poem of promise: the blind shall see, the
lame walk, the hungry will be fed, the sorrowing consoled,
and tears wiped from the land. "Nothing is impossible" is
Jesus' legacy. Like the fig tree in the parable, Jesus ex-
pects us to fly in the face of the expected and produce
fruit out of season. You and I are made for the impossible.

May my imagination overcome death and despair
with new possibility.

Reflection/Discussion Questions

1. What thoughts and feelings surfaced during this reading?

2. What are you projecting that will eventually happen?
   Is it what you truly want to project?

3. What messages of despair and hate are children exposed to today?
   What can you do to reduce their exposure?

4. What messages of hope, of new possibilities are children exposed to today?
   What can you do to increase their exposure?

5. What possibilities can you imagine that will overcome death and despair?

6. Do you believe that what a person projects will eventually happen?
   Why or why not?

7. Are you part of a "poetic community that offers explosive, concrete, subversive, critical images around which people can reorganize their lives?"
   If not, is there one you can join or can you form one yourself?

8. Do you believe that everyone has a partial truth?
   Why or why not?

Action Suggestions

1. Practice "compassionate listening," especially with those you consider "the enemy."

2. Commit to repeating daily the phrase "Nothing is impossible; I am made for the impossible."

3. Daily envision a world of peace and nonviolence; project what you want to eventually happen. By your actions, make it happen.

4. Work with people and organizations that project messages of hope, new possibilities and a new social reality, especially to children.

May I risk reputation,
comfort and security
to bring this hope to the children.

May I risk reputation, comfort and security to bring this hope to the children.

Living the truth in your heart without compromise
brings kindness into the world.
Attempts at kindness that compromise your heart
cause only sadness.
—Anonymous 18th Century Monk

To save one life, it is as if you had saved the world.
—Talmud

The Master gives himself up
to whatever the moment brings.
He knows that he is going to die,
and he has nothing left to hold on to,
no illusions of the mind,
no resistances in his body.
He doesn't think about his actions;
they flow from the core of his being.
He holds nothing back from life;
therefore he is ready for death,
as a man is ready for sleep
after a good day's work.
—Lao Tzu

The heart that breaks open can contain the whole universe.
—Joanna Rogers Macy

There is a lovely Talmudic story that when the children of Israel reached the Red Sea and Moses struck his staff on the shore, the waters and the sea did not part to let them through. The Israelites stood there at the edge of the water and nothing happened. Finally one of the men plunged into the sea. Then the waters rolled back.

The Nonviolent Moment

May I risk reputation, comfort and security
to bring this hope to the children.

During World War II a German widow hid Jewish refugees in her home. As her friends discovered the situation, they became extremely alarmed.

"You are risking your own well-being," they told her.

"I know that," she said.

"Then why," they demanded, "do you persist in this foolishness?"

Her answer was stark and to the point. "I am doing it," she said, "because the time is now and I am here."

—Source Unknown

Life shrinks or expands according to one's courage.
—Anais Nin

People who make no noise are dangerous.
—La Fontaine

If I had been asked in the first years of my spiritual life endeavor what I wanted people to say in appreciation of me, I would have answered, "Let them say, he is a holy man." Years later I would have answered, "Let them say he is a loving man." And now I would like people to say of me, "He is a free man."

—Anthony De Mello

May I risk reputation, comfort and security
to bring this hope to the children.

Reflection/Discussion Questions

1. What thoughts and feelings surfaced during these readings?

2. Which reading evoked the strongest response?
   Why?
   What does it say about where you are on the journey?

3. What is the truth in your heart?
   Are you living it without compromise?
   If not, what do you need to do to begin?

4. What do your actions say about the core of your being?

5. What hope are you bringing to the children in your family,
   community, country and world?

Action Suggestions

1. Commit daily to performing acts of hope, especially
   for the children.

2. Pray for the grace to be courageous, to hold nothing back
   from life.

Pax Christi USA

In a world that settles differences by armed violence and defines "justice" as "revenge," Pax Christi USA dares to break the cycle of violence by fostering reconciliation.

Pax Christi USA is the national Catholic peace movement reaching over half a million individuals in the United States. Our membership includes more than 550 religious communities, 450 parishes, 250 local groups, 130 U.S. bishops, 60 campus groups, and 19 regions that coordinate activities in their geographic areas.

The work of Pax Christi USA begins in personal life and extends to communities of reflection and action to transform structures of society. Pax Christi USA rejects war and every form of violence and domination. It advocates primacy of conscience, economic and social justice and respect for creation. Pax Christi USA commits itself to peace education and, with the help of its bishop members, promotes the gospel imperative of peacemaking as a priority in the Catholic Church in the United States. Through the efforts of all its members and in cooperation with other groups, Pax Christi USA works toward a more peaceful, just and sustainable world.

Pax Christi USA is a section of Pax Christi International, the Catholic peace movement.

Regular membership is $35 per year, entitling the subscriber to Pax Christi USA's bimonthly publication, the *Catholic Peace Voice,* and regular membership mailings. Full membership benefits are extended to those living on limited incomes who cannot afford the entire membership fee. For information about Pax Christi USA or to receive a free catalogue of our publications and sale items, please contact the national office.

Pax Christi USA
532 W. Eighth St.
Erie, PA 16502-1343
814-453-4955
Fax: 814-452-4784
info@paxchristiusa.org
www.paxchristiusa.org

About the Author

Mary Lou Kownacki, a Benedictine Sister of Erie, PA, is executive director of the Inner-City Neighborhood Art House in Erie and director of Benetvision, a resource center for contemporary spirituality. She served as national coordinator of Pax Christi USA from 1986 to 1991 and was named an Ambassador of Peace for Pax Christi. She has lived and worked in inner-city Erie for over 30 years, and has been instrumental in developing programs that serve the neighborhood. Sister Mary Lou has written extensively on the spirituality of nonviolence and has given retreats on the subject. She also leads writing workshops and teaches poetry to children at the Neighborhood Art House.

About the Artist

Helen David Brancato, IHM, is the art center director at the Southwest Community Enrichment Center in Philadelphia. Helen David has illustrated a number of books including *Walk with Jesus* by J.M. Nouwen and *Why Not Become Fire? Encounters with Women Mystics* by Evelyn Mattern.